FIRE
AND
FLOURISHING

FIRE AND FLOURISHING

POEMS

Kassi Wilson

Copyright © 2024 by Kassi Wilson

First paperback edition May 2024

Book design by Vanessa Mendozzi
Interior design by Vanessa Mendozzi

ISBN 979-8-9901099-0-2

www.kassiwilson.com

For Liz

Flare up like flame
and make big shadows I can move in.

If we surrendered
to earth's intelligence
we could rise up rooted, like trees.

- RAINER MARIA RILKE

Eden's slow unfolding
asks me to set aside
my rushed and useful life
to know myself as ripening.

- CHRISTINE VALTERS PAINTNER

CONTENTS

PART ONE

DEAR WORLD

I'm writing you a sympathy card,
though struggling for the right words
to put down. How does one say *get well*
with sincerity to a world so resistant
to getting better? A year ago I quit
watching the news cold turkey as I
couldn't stomach one more report on
death, loss, and destruction. Don't you
understand the hurt and pain so many
of us are feeling right now? Maybe you
don't know. I'm going to write anyways
and hope with all my heart things turn
around. Praying for brighter days—
may you mend, rest up, get well soon.

DAYS ARE LONG

I almost lost you.

Wait a minute I did lose you
during the hurry of the week
full of kids & carseats, stroller
walks downtown, school drop-
offs, bedtime routines, dirty
dishes & laundry, scrambled
eggs for dinner, no sitter.

Our years slowly accumulating
the way film overlays a glass-
paned window in Summer's
sticky heat. You were *with me*
& I locked my heart away
even though I missed you.

THE DESERT

Somewhere inside myself my soul
found solace in a desert of my own making.

My soul dragged her feet along labyrinth ground
—grainy, parched, dusty.

My soul swept her hands across blonde grass tips
flickering faintly in the wind.

My soul sizzled in the heat of day bearing down
under pressure she traversed in circles.

Stretches of time passed...
my soul taught me *my own* inner wandering.

WILDFIRES

I thought it was the increase in wildfires, traffic on 17, cost of living were my reasons for wanting to leave. Maybe it was the pandemic, schools closing, quarantine. Or cancer and surgery that left a scar on your throat. Maybe being isolated for months as the distance between us simmered inside our crumbling stucco house.

I think we both knew, we were more than ready for a change of scenery.

FLOURISHING

Has more to do with faith than ease
not giving up on love as love
upends every expectation.
Holding onto hope
even as the world despairs.
Notice gravity is both
friend & foe, keeps our toes
on the ground
yet obstacles abound.

Sometimes in my imagination
I'm pushing a boulder
up a steep hill
heaving with all my might.
If I stop halfway
any progress I gain
rolls away.

Anyhow, what am I
aiming for? Progress is
always a moving
target.

DIG DEEP

All I want on a day like today
is my hands in dirt. Digging in.
Transplant my cresting hostas
near the stone steps where light
splashes low. I have ferns drying
out and ivy crossing the fence.
I have rows of tiger lilies perking
awake in the shade, any day now
will flower—fiery gold flames.
Something in me knows tending
runs deep, throbs in my veins.
Something in me knows
as I care for mother earth
love grows.

WHILE ON A WALK

We need to see
    wings soar
fog rising over the ridge
catching daylight

We need to see
    roots & moss
plump robins digging up
stubborn worms

We need to see
    branches twirl
in the wind, spacious horizons
awakening new dreams

We need to see
    moody sunsets
casting flame & surprise
transfiguring wearied eyes

We need to see
    unending fields
with nowhere to be
nothing to prove.

FOR THE LOVE OF SUMMER

Crisp leaves fall in the air—

I stare in disbelief as golden trees still
gleam in the sun. Almost making it seem
Summer won't leave. Not now anyways,
I know it's coming. Shortly branches will
drop brittle leaves; gold foliage and leafy
ferns will wither in the cold. I'm not ready
to let go! It feels all is budding, bursting,
still blooming.

I need to say my goodbyes to every tree,
every leaf, and the fields bravely waving
even the grasses know it's time.

PART TWO

HANDKERCHIEFS

I find an old wooden box stored in a plastic bin and
begin to open—the box is filled with handkerchiefs
falling on my lap. Beautifully woven cloths embroidered
with bouquets or a single rose. I'm holding the cloths
in my hands and ask my mom, *why so many?* She answers.
The handkerchiefs belonged to your grandmother, it was
tradition to send a handkerchief with a sympathy card.
This detail piqued my curiosity since my mom barely
speaks of her—she remains a mystery. As the story
goes my grandmother had a mental break down when
my mom was a baby, a severe case of postpartum
depression, the details blur after this. She's diagnosed
with schizophrenia and admitted to a state hospital for
round-the-clock care. In the 50s my grandfather had
minimal options. It's hard to imagine what transpired,
details are lost in time. We know her life wasted away
in an institution absent and medicated. Her handkerchiefs
now antiques, folded and creased, tucked out of sight
until I open a forgotten box now my questions won't stop.

VAN GOGH STREET

If I chose a color for the latter half
of my thirties it would be gray, cloud-
gray billowing all over including the paint
of our interior walls. I opened the curtains
but for some odd reason blue skies rarely
showed. No matter what I tried I couldn't
part the clouds. As if cunning, the weather
kept the sunshine on the other side of town.
I can't get those seasons back. At least I had
sense to take road trips to the coast, foaming
waves slow and somber matched my mood.
Immersed in a wide open expanse I didn't
feel so cramped. And lively seagulls
were good company with outstretched
wings catching the tide winds.

UNDERSTORY

In the dark of dirt a seed
sends out its shoots.

Grows by heaving upward
pushing bit by bit.

Expands till breaching grass
to the skies' great mass.

What will a seed on the cusp
of change, who will it be

when breaking through
to a blue expanse?

SINS OF OMISSION

- Waiting for motivation to change
- Avoiding vulnerability
- Keeping the peace
- Self-Sabotage
- Not speaking up
- Accepting mediocrity
- Growing numb
- Slim intuition
- Lacking fierceness
- Failing to feel
- Insulating my heart

I NOTICE THE BLUE BOTTLE

On the counter beside your toothbrush
per instructions; Take 1 tablet every morning
ordered by the surgeon.

One pill a day, lifeline for you and new routine
before breakfast.

I still can't get over what you said late one night
your words still turn in my head. You didn't feel
I was there for you when you needed me.

Still baffled as to where my mind was, and how
I became so absent with something so important.

FACING FEAR

Don't trust someone who says *I don't have any fears.*

Your fears are what you don't want to look at—

what you avoid like the plague.

HARD CONVERSATION

The conversation you need to have
is almost always the one you don't
want to have. If you value honesty,
transparency over self-preservation
you'd be having the conversation(s).
And maybe it won't be so impossible.
It could be as simple as the activities
you do each day: gardening, jogging,
washing the dishes. What once was
unthinkable, out of your mind hard
becomes second nature. Natural as
breathing in and out.

MIRAGE

I admit, I romanticize life, always
bright-eyed in search of beauty

     gloss over the real world.

I can't pretend anymore.
Most days I'm fatigued, so needy,
and clouds hunched low in the sky
dangle like a giant mirror mocking
the speckled pavement.

POETRY 101

If you want to have a sane life, a pragmatic life—
resist the urge to reach for a pen to write poetry.

It will open Pandora's box

                    how could it not!

But if something in you is dying to write and the
blank page beckons, get a pen, see what happens.

PART THREE

REDWOODS

Peak wildfire season is July through October,
our last months in California. The thought of
fire reaching the redwoods never a pleasant
image—evergreens rooted in mountains
having lived a thousand years.

Westerly winds sent smoke in all directions
        making it hard to breathe.

Smoke stuck to the valley sky...till finally...

Wildfires died-down, autumn rains watered
        acres of scorched woods.

I imagine in my dreams a conifer seed
cracking open, moss healing the forest floor,
a dove piercing the misty air
with her solemn voice—

light glittering a soft glow
        blessing the ground of resilient land.

INVISIBLE TEARS

The fight last night wasn't about lighting
candles in the house. It wasn't about holiday
decorating or accessible fire extinguishers.
The fight wasn't about a five-foot grease fire
flaring out of control when you were young.
In the middle of back & forth, smoke & mirrors
I see your eyes, I see fear, I see it welling up—
you doubt love.

There are mornings a pot of coffee
is stability getting us through.

UNLEASH

I feel rage stirring inside—
deep emotion releasing anger

unleashing compassion. Rage
doesn't happen in a vacuum.

It's passed down stealthily

one generation to the next till
someone's great, great, great

granddaughter no longer has
a stoic code of conduct.

SPARKS FLY

A fire lights

    inside.

Pure love

    its only fuel.

I won't let it

    go out,

not now,

    not ever.

GLIMPSE

Sometimes I catch myself observing
my life from an aerial view. I peer above
my tiny existence and see myself moving
about, flittering to here, flittering to there
in open air as a hummingbird. Heart
beating fast hovering over every yellow
circle at the center of every flower. This
gives me essential distance from my life
up-close and a larger picture gives way
to the magic all around. But no matter
how many times I steal a glimpse and look,
there's a thin fog shielding the great mystery
over the whole of existence. It makes me
crazy desperate to know the core of reality.
The heat of life at the center of it all.

BLAST TO THE PAST

Reading old cards you wrote the sweetest
love notes, so in love, infatuation off the charts.
You thought I was perfect. I thought you were
perfect too. Through the years the pedestals
we put ourselves on came down. Dismantled
by its fake glory and broken promises.

Now we live as two people, perfectly flawed,
hungry for love and eager to be known
for who we are—

you as you, me as me.

TO BE 17 AGAIN

Seventeen—so fun, cartwheels on the lawn,
car rides between our houses, quick pitstops
buying sodas, brownies for later, cucumbers
and peach scrub for facials.

Summer days blurred together like fireworks
bursting in blooms just talking under the stars
not weighed down, good feelings grew on trees.

Stayed up all night watching Happy Gilmore,
Pride & Prejudice. We could turn a boring day
into anything we wanted to because it was us.
We were better together than if we were apart.

Sang Shania country at the top of our lungs
with conviction, like we knew what it would feel
like to be a woman. Little did we know—
how it all would change, how everything changes.

MULTIPLE SELVES

Another year around the sun

belonging to earth & its beautiful
unfolding.

I know myself
at age ten wonder in her eyes
at fifteen all energy living larger than life
at twenty-two aimless, naive, just beginning
at thirty a new mom loving life & loathing life
all at once.

There's my other self *with me* all this time
contemplative & mysterious dialed in
to a knowing depth.

Wiser than my years, slowly revealing who she is.

WINTER LESSONS

In the night fog rolled in like a down
blanket over the grass, frostbitten by
the cold. The rooms in my house still
asleep. Outside my window clouds break
away unveiling blue consoling skies. Rows
of sparrows perch among pine branches,
cardinals flutter between the trees. Frost
covered rooftops sparkle in the light.
The lessons this season are simple.

1. Sit awhile
2. Rest
3. Be at peace

NEW CHAPTER

You settle into a house with good bones
and some potential. Then change comes
knocking at your sea-blue door still
smelling of fresh paint. You pack your
belongings once again and follow the turn
in tide—it leads you to a new place to call
home. So you unpack your entire life and
start again. You are the same woman,
same flaws, same old hurdles to overcome
but as fate would have it—you feel new.
Something's shifted in you, when looking
at yourself in the mirror your own reflection
wants to show you, you've changed. See,
you've changed! And this time it's better than
you ever could have envisioned.

Alive!

As you're breaking down
walls and your hair flows free
in the wind.

As you're walking out of
rooms that kept you small and
overly confined.

Don't be surprised if egos
shatter and very few get you.

Keep the celebration going
even if balloons pop one by one
and the orange punch is poured
out—the good girl persona
never suited you.

PART FOUR

As the Birds

When the going gets tough

    don't shrink back

in your dream pursuit.

    You're not walking on

a linear path of forward progress.

    Getting there is cyclical,

the way a bird catches

    the wind and soars in open air.

If the wind was absent in helping

    the bird along...

she wouldn't be capable

    of soaring to new heights.

As the birds

you're going to need

supernatural wind

to move your wings.

WAKING AT DAWN

Some days she wakes early
before anyone makes a stir.

Brews a pot of coffee, sips
slow like—letting steam rise.

She cracks open a window
just to hear the crickets hum.

She lets the rhythm remind her
of things forgotten, of mysteries

that make our world spin.

WHERE HAS THE WILD GONE

Where did the woodpeckers go to,
the foxes, the wolves, the hawks
swooping from the trees,
deer and their majestic antlers.

Where are oaks and their acorn
offerings along the way,
grasses and reeds drumming
as waves in the near distance.

Where is wisdom, lost parables
from long ago, the stories we hunger
to hear that would break us in two,
rupture our flesh—

while bleeding with pierced hearts
we rise back to life.

FIRST FEMALE SCIENTIST

She was bright and curious. When she wasn't tending
to her peonies and rose bushes, Eve went gallivanting
in paradise observing every living thing. She knew
the names of all the animals, plants, floras, and seeds.
Everything she could see was classified and memorized
by heart. So when a strange creature waltzes its scaly
body with pointy teeth and shifty eyes through the hedge
groves she wonders to herself...what's this? Adam was
somewhere swinging in the trees so she decides to figure
out this perplexing puzzle. She thought she studied every
bird and reptile but this isn't a reptile. Its mouth opens,
begins talking, now she's confused. Feeling uneasy for
the first time in her life—Eve is famished. She reaches
for the closest fruit bearing tree and takes a bite.

PLAY YARD

You are near your son, a smile graces
your face while you watch him explore
the play yard. I look again and notice
your tired eyes. I'm only passing through
but I know how it is. Weeks are full while
you daydream of what your life could be
and all you hope to do. You are in between
worlds, the one you're in, precious and close.
And the wider world out there.

Daydream, still dream, only don't let it
narrow the present. Your own life blossoms
even now.

ABSENCE OF HEAT

On a chilly morning
    my son tells me

the cold isn't cold, that really
    cold is the absence of heat.

Absence interesting…
    the wheels in my head turn.

I'm learning a physics lesson
    and for the first time it's hitting me.

So heat is something, it exists.
    Then the cold can't be considered

something because it's the absence of something.
Cold can't even be

heat's nemesis. So the effect of heat
being distant in proximity feels cold: cold is absence.

I shiver thinking about my absentee relatives—
the grandmothers, the aunts, the uncle and his tragic death.

RUNNING ON FUMES

My soul aren't you tired, haven't you been here before
circling parched land?

The lives we build are shallow tilling at the surface—
chasing shiny things, petty things, numbing inner need,
running from dullness, boredom, restlessness.

My soul aren't you tired, haven't you been here before
circling?

Haven't you seen enough what people do to cover pain
and emptiness. See how modern life resembles our thirsty
condition, when earth is abundantly watered.

My soul aren't you tired?

WILL YOU WANT ME?

When wrinkles line my face, when my hair is mostly gray holding me as you do now? The present passes without our permission. I want to believe fate can't be callous, that our love outlasts breath, that it won't vanish in the end. Yet seasons march forward as rivers funnel to the ocean floor. Our days flicker as fireflies against a half-moon, august fades in autumn's crisp winds unveiling imminent change. Brings me to my knees... shedding of leaves, compost for bonfires lit beneath the stars. Smoke rising in the distant cold.

IGNITION

It's your average kind of day—sunlight is glossy
in the sky flatlining the horizon and I'm walking
into every room of my house looking for car keys
I can't find. I frantically turn over cushions open
drawers and feeling unsettled, I notice an ache
in my chest. The ache and my heart coexist
seem inseparable. What am I searching for?
When I find my keys start the ignition and drive.
What if I drive all over searching…?
I worry about my condition, the ache, my grief.
I wonder if my grief is proof of God.

Staring Down Fear

I used to think my fears were the silly kind, the kind you'd laugh about at a dinner party, fears like snakes or swimming in open water with tiger sharks lurking down below. Over the years my fears have matured. I fear being alone for too long or walking in thick fog when the surrounding trees grow surreal. I realize now I hate the cold late at night and the only warmth you feel is steam from your own breath. Yet my fears go deeper than these things, more layered and hard to grasp on a conscious level. Sometimes I fear my inner-critic...the voice in my mind. Voices eroding confidence that steal my freedom and my joy. Voices deflating self-worth. Voices fired up even fueled by deep-seated insecurities. For reasons I don't understand I'm relating to my grandmother's story—its devastating sadness. She heard voices and it seemed crazy. Did her condition warrant a sentence in a mental institution? Separated from family and society? I'll never know. It's tiresome hearing the same platitudes. Something I wonder is... we fear the things we don't understand about ourselves and others, we fear what we might find lurking inside the rooms of our minds. Those deemed crazy are put away in a brick building and by a twist of fate the public is dealt a pass to not have to really see another's pain. I've been dealt the same pass, look the other way and mask what ails me. Although I know my wounds give me away and I bleed.

PART FIVE

WHEN YOU BECOME A MOM

No one tells you part of your life is given away
handed over in your prime. That days...nights...
will be consumed with feeding, caring, nurturing.
You'll settle into sleep only to be startled back
awake by piercing cries—your baby needs you.
No one tells you that your hips will grow, jeans
won't feel the same anymore, feet lose their arch.
No one tells you of the brain-numbing hours
over dirty floors picking up toys and cheerios.
That dinner will be whatever you conjure up,
a hot meal on the table by 6pm is miraculous.
No one tells you during the darkest nights you'll
wonder if your life is yours, if you'll dream again.

In the middle of it all you're not alone—
you'll make it through, you will, you'll see!

TENDING + TENDING

I Live My Days Tending

I write words,
    I write lines,
        I tend to my life.

Omitting a letter, snipping stanzas, replacing
a period with a comma, pruning.

    Tending truly as I can,
though lacking the precision of a master gardener.

What do I tend that won't crumble in a river only to
cycle-thru & wash away? As bitter winds blow or storms
cast hail uprooting the good being sown, what then?

    It feels feeble and still beauty unraveling
breaches the surface in places sun dawns
and rain falls on fallow ground.

Plans may fail,
efforts might not yield a thing.
By faith, by faith
    I'm not the only one
        tending.

BOYHOOD

My son sits next to me and shares
his ideas without pausing to breathe.
Imagination running full speed—
worlds and stories burst into existence.
Bedroom filled with sketches taped floor
to ceiling. Striking creatures, maps, tales of
lost folklore. Excitement materializing.
I'm in total awe: his peers are on Snapchat
scrolling, texting, don't bother with imaginary
play, on their phones, all grownup.

FLASHES OF BEAUTY

Woke up
and hurried downstairs
for a glass of water. I almost turned on
the kitchen lights but stopped to look
outside. The sky wore a hypnotizing color—
red like embers smoldering inside a campfire.
I stood there gazing at its billowing brightness
fade behind a gray veil. There's a certain
irony to this, our experience of the beautiful
comes and goes.

Beauty is like a guest from another place
very much present in our world. In the everyday
rinse and repeat of our lives flashes of beauty waken
our senses, elevating our spirits. Beauty is a language
and her words are not foreign to us. A voice we viscerally
know but vaguely recall. Beauty seeks our attention
and enchants us, both faces of the coin flip and flip,
a message being sent and received.

STRAWBERRY FLAVORED SUNSETS

Remember when
you loved to crimp your hair and it
stayed a tangled mess for days.

Remember purple leggings,
pierced earrings, baggy shirts...

VHS tapes, Disney movies on repeat.
You knew all the lyrics, sang out loud,
performed for no one.

Remember swimming at the beach
diving deep like a mermaid because
you believed you were a mermaid.

Remember carpe diem summers
lost in play, only pausing long enough
to watch the sun as it set...

your gaze drew in every pink hue,
every last texture and gleam of light.

Before the sky darkened and you
turned to walk home.

ORANGE POPPIES

In my mind's eye I still see July blooms
dancing in the fields—hiking through
chaparral hills climbing mid the skies.
I felt in my spirit a feeling of gratitude
for the gift of sight. My eyes fit for taking
in color utterly alive and fiery as orange.
The year prior a woman came to these
mountainside fields holding a canvas
pouch she carried at her hip. We crossed
paths midway on a trail. I smiled hello,
walked on till reaching a higher vantage
and quickly turned to see her scattering
seeds—swaying in a field of dry grass.
Here I am going about my day catching
a rare glimpse since occurrences like this
are not common. I fumbled into the scenery
as a witness yet what was being witnessed?
Maybe that day I saw something spectacular,
a sliver of the infinite, a thrill of freedom
that accompanies a woman when stepping
out to play. Whether there to see it or not
never mattered. I enjoyed the poppies.

TREES ARE LOSING LEAVES

And I must be losing
my wits or will to go on
feeling as though
I'm losing all hope. And as
leaves fall in slow surrender,
I too am falling, more like flailing
mid gusty winds getting
colder every day.
I want to make the best of things
but all is frail inside a world bursting
apart. My heart overfills
with mounting
despair palpable in the atmosphere.
And so before the ground
freezes over I plant
what little hope is left. Bury it
deep in dirt close to worms, withering
fruit, samara seeds, crushed
acorns. Then wait, longingly
endure the cold. For now
my hope hides
layered...
under frostbitten leaves.

SUDDEN SPRING

A miracle happened
    as the sun, daybreak

in our house. Lighting up windows
    dancing over floorboards.

Buds popping out amid
    our comings & goings,

subtle change growing.
    Walls unfurling plumeria,

orchids, gardenia, evergreen ivy
    lacing mantels & doorhandles.

A fragrant breeze swept
    all through our halls.

EARTH

Offers Herself To You

Is she a plateau to spoil and plunder?

If earth were a flat thing, a functional thing.
If the ground was made of clay, no life could be
scraped away, disfigured, or ruined beyond repair.

All of earth is garden even desert sands grow
living things and prickly cactuses bloom flowers,
forests, coral reefs, prairies, and valleys, all gardens.

Earth knows her truth, mankind is confused. And
concerning Eve, who is she? The mother of all living,
every woman is a daughter of Eve.

Something like scales cover her light. If only all could see
her potential, wisdom, gentle ways. Earth and Eve
are one—her flourishing brings healing.

OLD STORY

If my heart is
a mirror to yours
I know how the story
goes.

The world will make
you forget raining burdens,
misery and disappointment.

But heartache doesn't ruin us.

We fall asleep go numb without
ever flinching. Happens just by
living...the heart failing to feel.

From one heart to another
there's no fast cure, somehow
our hearts will heal...

But how you might say?

Start by waking slowly
and as the sky widens
like a balm of light
let it save you
every time.

FULL CIRCLE

When you realize there's no arrival point
and each day you wake, you start over.

The dark filling the night sky is earth's
rinse cycle that washes the day clean.

Morning dew, leftover residue.

After a long night of sleep, temporarily
forgetting everything like amnesia—

you wake to a fresh start.

THE CHASM

My dreams appeared distant...

gaping chasm up ahead between the place
I was and where I wanted to go. Doubting
if I had the talent, the knowhow to make
a way across. Seasons came and went, my
wishing turned to daydreams musings of
the mind. Maybe when dreams are not
pursued they go dormant as foliage wither
in the dead of winter and life in all its color
loses luster. Maybe it's better like this, still
hoping to be known for who I am, but
how could I know myself being stuck in
the same place? Looking over its ledge...
the chasm echoed back my fears. I tried
ignoring it with the whims of the day, its
many demands. Checking off lists, every
little task, waking sleepily to the next day
while I groaned, *there must be more*. Toyed
with an image of myself, risk adverse, self-
limitation kept me tightly wound. It could
have stayed like this, yet one chance day
the winds blew carrying a gentle whisper.
In a moment I muster the courage to leap
to my surprise I grow wings fierce as fire.

LIFE IS

Don't tell me
the sky looks drab these days
sunlight dims a little more every day
Don't tell me
beauty won't last
as fireflies flickering out at midnight
Don't tell me
a house sparrow went extinct
her birdsong now available on audio
Don't tell me
good in the world wanes
as if virtue was only for yesterday
Don't tell me
all men have gone weak
fold to their knees in the face of evil
Don't tell me
the young are lost
were never taught right from wrong
Don't tell me
to drink my sorrow in shots of vodka
since time a vale of tears
Don't tell me
A.I. makes a poet's voice
obsolete

Don't spoil everything droning on
about the end of things

as long as I have breath

let me suspend   disbelief
let me still believe   life is beautiful

ACKNOWLEDGMENTS

Thank you family and friends for reading my poems and offering invaluable feedback. I want to thank my husband for your love and belief in my dream pursuits. There's no one I'd rather share this life with. Thank you to my creative boys with big imaginations—you inspire me every day. Thank you Vanessa Mendozzi for the beautiful cover and interior design.

I included a few quotes from Rilke's Book of Hours: Love Poems to God. And a quote from Christine Valters Paintner's poem "Ripening" that came from her book Dreaming of Stones.

This poetry book is dedicated to grandmother Dorothy and the memory of her life.

Dear reader

Thank you for reading fire and flourishing. If you enjoyed this collection of poems you will also like my debut poetry book—Growing Gills: Poems. Available for purchase on Amazon and major online bookstores.

Let's stay in touch!

Instagram @kassiwilsonpoet
Email hello@kassiwilson.com
Website kassiwilson.com

Printed in the USA
CPSIA information can be obtained
at www.ICGtesting.com
LVHW040325190524
780461LV00006B/699

9 798990 109902